KANSAS

Past and Present

Diane Bailey

rosen publishing's
rosen
central®

New York

Published in 2011 by The Rosen Publishing Group, Inc.
29 East 21st Street, New York, NY 10010

First Edition

Library of Congress Cataloging-in-Publication Data

Bailey, Diane, 1966–
Kansas: past and present / Diane Bailey. — 1st ed.
    p. cm. — (The United States: past and present)
Includes bibliographical references and index.
ISBN 978-1-4358-9481-5 (library binding)
ISBN 978-1-4358-9508-9 (pbk.)
ISBN 978-1-4358-9542-3 (6-pack)
1. Kansas—Juvenile literature. I. Title.
F681.3.B35 2011
978.1—dc22

2010000816

Manufactured in Malaysia

CPSIA Compliance Information: Batch #S10YA: For further information, contact Rosen Publishing, New York, New York, at 1-800-237-9932.

On the cover: Top left: Settlers from the eastern states flowed onto the Kansas prairie in the 1800s. Top right: The Boeing Company constructs aircraft at factories in Wichita. Bottom: This golden wheat is ready for harvest in a field in Kansas.

Contents

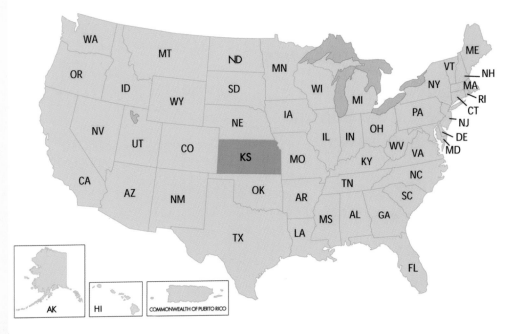

Most residents of Kansas live in cities in the eastern half of the state. Located in the center of the continental United States, Kansas is considered part of the Midwest.

Introduction

People sometimes say that Kansas is in "the middle of nowhere." Actually, Kansas is in the middle of everywhere! The geographic center of the mainland United States (the part that does not include Alaska or Hawaii) is in northeast Kansas. Kansas is a day's drive from both Mexico and Canada. And of course, it's only a short tornado ride to Oz.

Kansas is shaped like a graham cracker with a nibble out of the northeast corner. The eastern and western parts of Kansas are very different. The west is flat, dry plains. The east gets more rain and is filled with trees. The first white explorers and settlers often did not know what to make of the Kansas landscape. Those who saw the east thought it was beautiful. Others, traveling through the west, thought it was a wasteland that would never be good for farming.

Native Americans lived in Kansas for thousands of years. Many of them hunted buffalo that roamed in huge herds. In the mid-1800s, white settlers started to arrive. Residents of Kansas then had a big question to answer: Would it be a slave state or a free state? Supporters on both sides arrived by the thousands, trying to tip the balance.

Kansans chose not to allow slavery, a decision that affected the entire United States. Meanwhile, the state's economy exploded through wheat, oil, and aviation. Drive down a Kansas highway and you'll see signs that read, "One Kansas farmer feeds 128 people and you." Look beyond the signs, and you'll see how all Kansans have helped build their state and their country.

Chapter 1

THE GEOGRAPHY OF KANSAS

"Shark!" If you are in Kansas and someone yells that, don't panic. It's probably just a paleontologist who has found a fossil. Sharks don't live in Kansas anymore, but about seventy million years ago, they did. Kansas was underwater then. Thousands of creatures lived in this warm and shallow sea, including sharks and mosasaurs, which were huge marine reptiles. Now fossils of these animals are found in the layers of rock that cover Kansas. That huge sea evaporated a long time ago. Now Kansas has another kind of sea—one made out of grass. If you weighed all the different plants in Kansas separately, the winner would be grass!

The Land

Most people's image of Kansas comes from the landscape in the western half of the state. These are the high plains. Miles of short grasses cover this flat land. There is little water. Few trees stop the powerful winds in this part of the state.

To the east of the high plains are the Smoky Hills. This region is filled with ancient limestone and sandstone. Settlers often built things from limestone because it was easier to find than wood. South of the Smoky Hills are the Red Hills. These hills have ribbons of iron oxide, or rust, which gives them their reddish-brown coloring.

The short grasses of the west give way to a mixed-grass prairie in the central part of the state and finally into tall grasses in parts of the east. The Flint Hills in the south-east are covered by the tallgrass prairie but have rocks underneath the surface. It was a difficult place to farm, especially with metal plows.

The eastern third of Kansas is hilly and green. The Osage Cuestas cover most of the southeast quarter. Northeast Kansas is known as the Glaciated Region. Between one and two million years ago, glaciers moved across this area. They left behind huge boulders after they melted and cut new waterways through the land.

An enormous prehistoric fish from the Cretaceous period, one hundred million years ago, was found in Kansas in the 1920s.

The Missouri River forms the northeastern border of Kansas. The Kansas River, also called the Kaw River, flows into the Missouri. The Arkansas River travels across the southwestern part of the state to eventually drain into the Mississippi River.

Amazing rock formations can be seen in Kansas. Castle Rock is a tower of limestone that rises almost 70 feet (21 meters) from a flat

The Tallgrass Prairie

The tallgrass prairie once covered hundreds of miles of the United States. It reached south to Texas and north into Canada. "Tall" means tall: These grasses, including varieties called big bluestem, little bluestem, and Indian grass, can grow between 8 and 9 feet (2 and 3 m) high.

The tallgrass prairie was important to Indians who lived in Kansas before white people arrived. The buffalo they ate lived by grazing in this prairie. For a tallgrass prairie to thrive, it actually has to be destroyed. The best way to do this is by fire. The burned plants put nutrients back into the ground. Also, fire kills non-native species that could hurt the prairie. Indians would burn the prairie to improve grazing for buffalo and make traveling easier. When cattle became big business in Kansas, cowboys drove their herds through the prairie to fatten the cows before they were sold.

As settlers moved in, farmers plowed up much of the tallgrass prairie to use it for growing crops. Today, only about 2 percent of this prairie remains nation-wide. In 1996, a preserve was formed to save more than 10,000 acres (4,047 hectares) of tallgrass prairie in the Flint Hills of Kansas. In 2005, the Nature Conservancy bought the land and now operates it along with the National Park Service. In 2008, the preserve was named one of the "eight wonders of Kansas." The region's history in the cattle industry is alive and well. Cattle still graze on the prairie before they go to market. The Nature Conservancy is also planning to reintroduce buffalo. This little slice of Kansas looks much like it did two hundred years ago.

plain in the Smoky Hills. More of these pillars can be found at Monument Rocks, also known as the Chalk Pyramids. Giant sandstone boulders can be viewed at Rock City, and mushroom-shaped rock towers stand at Mushroom Rock State Park.

Strong winds blow through the wide-open plains of western Kansas, turning windmills that help pump water to farms. On wind farms, this energy helps generate electricity for the state.

Climate

People in Kansas joke that the weather changes every five minutes. If you visited Kansas in March, you might need snow boots and a scarf, or you might need shorts and sunscreen.

In March 1899, the town of Harper, Kansas, had a tornado. The town also got rain, ice, sleet, and snow—and a beautiful sunset. That was all within twenty-four hours!

Extreme weather is normal in Kansas. Blizzards can rage in the winter. Spring brings tornadoes. They blow up from Texas and Oklahoma, gaining speed over the empty plains of western Kansas as they move in a northeast direction across the state. Kansas's tornadoes were made famous in the movie *The Wizard of Oz*, when a twister took Dorothy on her adventure. In real life, Kansas gets fewer tornadoes than Texas and Oklahoma, but they can be just as bad. In 2007, a tornado devastated the southern town of Greensburg.

Spring brings tornadoes that can level houses and even entire towns in only a few minutes. Here, victims sort through the debris left behind by a tornado that struck Greensburg in 2007, destroying much of the town.

The state is known for cold winters and hot summers. The highest temperature ever recorded in Kansas was 121 degrees Fahrenheit (49 degrees Celsius). That's about as hot as it gets in Death Valley, the hottest place in the United States. It has also gotten as cold as -40°F (-4°C), which is more like northern Canada.

Plants and Animals

The song "Home on the Range" talks about a land "where the buffalo roam." A Kansas man named Dr. Brewster A. Higley wrote the lyrics of that song. In the late 1800s, buffalo were hunted until they were almost extinct. The species recovered, but now buffalo in Kansas only live on preserves. In 1904, the last mountain lion was killed—at least that's what everyone thought. A hundred years later, in 2004, people began reporting that they had seen mountain lions. Footprints and photographs confirmed what they had said. However,

An adult bison (buffalo) and a calf roam on a prairie preserve. The animals provided food for early Kansans, and their grazing is important to the health of native prairie grasslands.

it is not known whether the animals were living in Kansas or entered from another state.

Today, the plains, forests, and rivers of Kansas are filled with a variety of animals, including beavers, badgers, foxes, deer, and bobcats. The musical western meadowlark (the state bird) likes the state's dry grasslands. Large birds, such as wild turkeys and bald eagles, can be found near streams and rivers. In the rivers of Kansas live freshwater mussels, sometimes called Kansas clams. Throughout the twentieth century, mussels were harvested to make pearl buttons. Now many mussel species in Kansas are threatened due to overharvesting and habitat loss.

Grasses—tall, short, and in between—cover thousands of acres in Kansas. Cottonwood trees grow throughout Kansas, and forests in the east have oak, hickory, and elm trees. One beautiful sight is a field of yellow sunflowers, which give the state its nickname.

Chapter 2

THE HISTORY OF KANSAS

In 1541, a Spanish explorer named Francisco Vásquez de Coronado came to Kansas looking for a city of gold. An Indian slave convinced Coronado that he knew where to find this city, called Quivira. Coronado followed the slave to present-day Wichita. But he did not find gold—only a dry land where he found it difficult to survive.

Native Peoples and Explorers

People have lived in Kansas for about thirteen thousand years. Early residents hunted mammoths and giant bison. From about 800 to 400 BCE, the Hopewell Indians lived in Kansas. They built huge ceremonial mounds and began to grow crops for food. By the time white explorers came in the 1500s, several Indian tribes called Kansas home, including the Osage, Wichita, and Pawnee. The state gets its name from the Kansa Indians, whose name means "people of the south wind."

In the 1800s, more explorers pushed through Kansas. The team of Meriwether Lewis and William Clark liked northeast Kansas. But explorer Zebulon Pike was not impressed. He described western Kansas as the "Great American Desert."

There were no highways in Kansas in the 1800s, but there was still a lot of traffic. The state was a popular route for settlers who were traveling west looking for new land and opportunities.

To get from the settled eastern states to the unexplored western territories, most travelers went through Kansas. The Santa Fe Trail crossed Kansas on its way from New Mexico to Missouri. Thousands of settlers passed through Kansas on the Oregon Trail. The Chisholm Trail was a route that cowboys used to herd cattle from Texas to Kansas. Many people were traveling across Kansas in the early 1800s. By the middle of the century, they were starting to stay there.

However, Native Americans and white people did not live well together. In the early nineteenth century, Indians in eastern states were pushed out to make room for white people. They were forced to go live in Kansas and other parts of the frontier. A half-century

Cowboy Culture

Cowboys drove huge herds of cattle—thousands at a time—up from Texas into the wide-open prairies of Kansas. Being a cowboy wasn't just a job. It was a whole culture that thrived from the 1860s to the 1880s. Cowboys spent months on the trail, braving bad weather and Indian attacks. The days were long and tiring. However, they entertained themselves with songs and stories about their homes and adventures.

At the end of the trail were the cities of Abilene, Wichita, and Dodge City. These fast-growing Kansas towns existed mostly to serve the beef industry. There were lots of men, lots of money, and lots of trouble. These cities became known as violent, lawless places where gunfights were common in saloons and in the streets.

In the 1900s, the cowboy culture began to die out. By about 1960, the huge railroad stockyards were being torn down. Cattle were moved on trucks instead of trains. Cows are still an important part of the Kansas economy. They are raised on ranches and in large feedlots. Their meat is cleaned, cut, and packaged at one of the state's huge packing facilities. Today's cowboys are more likely to drive pickup trucks, carry cell phones, and be home in time for dinner.

However, that past time still fascinates people. They like the excitement of the Wild West and the romance of sleeping under the stars. The culture lives on in museums and hands-on activities. Museums in Wichita and Dodge City show the details of cowboy life and the real Wild West. Tourists can even visit ranches where they can ride horses, eat around a campfire, and see how today's cowboys work.

later, when Kansas was opened up to white settlement, Indians were forced out again, mostly south into Oklahoma.

Bleeding Kansas

During the first half of the nineteenth century, the United States was sharply divided on the issue of slavery. The South produced a lot of crops, such as cotton and tobacco.

In this illustration, a group of proslavery forces from Missouri kills some "free-soiler" Kansas settlers who are in favor of abolition.

These were grown on huge farms called plantations. Black slaves did most of the work. However, northerners did not approve of slavery.

In 1854, the U.S. Congress passed the Kansas-Nebraska Act, which opened up this territory to white settlers. Under the law, people in this new area could decide whether or not to allow slavery. The territory was up for grabs.

Almost immediately, people began coming to Kansas, especially from the East. Some of them wanted to abolish, or get rid of, slavery. They were called abolitionists. They were also known as free-soilers or Jayhawkers. The northeast city of Lawrence was founded specifically for abolitionists. Proslavery people poured in from the South and from neighboring Missouri, a slave state.

Tensions arose between the two camps. In 1856, a group of proslavery men attacked Lawrence. A zealous Jayhawker named John

Brown led a revenge attack. The violence increased, and the region came to be known as Bleeding Kansas. By 1859, however, the Jayhawkers had won. Kansas was declared free.

Throughout 1860, Kansans worked to write a constitution. Three versions were rejected before one was finally agreed upon. On January 29, 1861, Kansas was admitted as the thirty-eighth state in the Union.

The fight over slavery still wasn't over, however. Only months after Kansas became a state, the country entered the Civil War. The North and the South fought bitterly, with slavery as the central issue. When President Abraham Lincoln called for troops in the Civil War, about two-thirds of the eligible men in Kansas (about twenty thousand) volunteered. Nearly half of them died. Kansas lost a larger percentage of men than any other state.

Although Kansas was not the site of any major Civil War battles, one bloody attack did make history. In 1863, Confederate (Southern) soldier William Quantrill stormed through Lawrence at dawn, killing 150 people and burning the city.

History books say that the Civil War began in 1861, but many believe it started earlier, in 1854, when the battle over Kansas began.

Growing a State

By the time the Civil War ended in 1865, the country had been torn apart. Farms and railroads had been ruined. People were exhausted from fighting. However, they could finally return to the progress that had started before the war. Railroads were built in Kansas. They made the western part of the state easier to reach and helped boost the economy. Buffalo were a problem, however. They were a nuisance to farmers and a danger to trains. The railroad hired buffalo hunters to kill the animals and provide food for workers. Other hunters went after the buffalo for sport. Within only a few years, buffalo were almost extinct.

After the Civil War, thousands of black Americans—especially freed slaves—moved to Kansas. In 1879, about six thousand southern blacks arrived. They were called Exodusters. Nicodemus, Kansas, was the first town west of the Mississippi River that was founded by black Americans.

Farming, especially wheat, became an important industry. Kansas thrived in the last part of the nineteenth century and the early part of the twentieth. However, in the 1930s, the state suffered during the Dust Bowl, when years of drought ruined many farms.

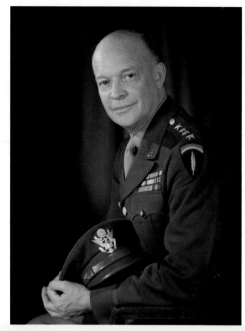

After his success as a five-star general during World War II in the early 1940s, Dwight D. Eisenhower, from Abilene, Kansas, was elected president in 1953 and served for two terms, until 1961.

When the United States entered World War II in 1941, Kansas helped support the thousands of troops fighting overseas. Kansas provided food, such as grains and beef, as well as airplane parts for the military. The state also gave the United States its top commander—General Dwight D. Eisenhower. Eisenhower came from Abilene, Kansas. In 1953, he was elected president.

The state has certainly lived up to its motto, *Ad astra per aspera,* which means "To the stars through difficulties."

Chapter 3

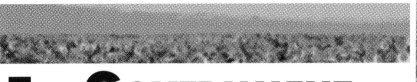

THE GOVERNMENT OF KANSAS

Kansas was ready to be admitted as a state in 1860, but it took until 1861. That year, several southern states seceded from the Union in advance of the Civil War. Those senators dropped out of Congress. That gave Kansas enough votes to be admitted as a free state.

Now that Kansas was an official state, there were many other decisions to make about its government.

The Structure of Government

Like the national government, Kansas's government is divided into three branches. The legislative branch makes laws. The executive branch makes sure the laws are carried out. It also oversees other services. The judicial branch deals with crimes and settles disputes.

The legislative branch of government has two parts, the senate and the house of representatives. Kansas has forty senators. Each serves a four-year term. The house has 125 members who serve 2-year terms. Kansas does not limit how many terms that legislators can serve. As long as the voters elect them, they can keep their offices.

The governor leads the executive branch. The governor signs bills into laws and supervises other departments. For example, there are departments for health and the environment, education, agriculture, commerce, wildlife and parks, transportation, and social services. The people who head these departments are part of the governor's cabinet. Cabinet members help the governor. A lieutenant governor serves under the governor. If the governor cannot finish his or her term, the lieutenant governor takes over. This happened in 2009, when Governor Kathleen Sebelius resigned to take a job in the administration of President Barack Obama. Lieutenant Governor Mark Parkinson took office.

The Kansas State Capitol in Topeka took thirty-seven years to build and cost $3.2 million. Today, that money would not even pay for the marble floor.

The judicial branch is organized into a system of courts. Minor cases are held in a municipal (local) court. More serious ones go to a district court. Sometimes cases are appealed. This means whoever lost the case asks for it to be tried again. The court of appeals hears these cases. The biggest cases go to the state's supreme court. These cases may be important criminal trials, or they might be about issues that affect the entire state, such as the rights of the state's citizens. There are seven justices (judges) on the supreme court.

Struggles in Schools

In the 1950s, white children went to different schools than black children. The parents of Linda Brown, an African American girl who lived in Topeka, protested. They joined with some other parents and filed a lawsuit against the board of education. At first the court sided with the school district, saying that schools for black children were as good as the schools the white children attended. Therefore, the state had not done anything illegal.

The case was appealed. In 1954, it went to the U.S. Supreme Court. The Supreme Court overturned the earlier decision. In a unanimous vote, the justices decided that the act of segregation was wrong. This ruling led to the integration of schools nationwide.

In 2005, the Kansas Board of Education faced a new issue. This time, it discussed what would be taught in high school science classes about the origin of human life. The theory of evolution, which states that humans evolved from other species of animals, was already taught in the schools. The board members wanted to introduce another theory: intelligent design. This theory essentially said that an intelligent being (God) created people.

Many scientists and citizens objected to this idea. They argued that intelligent design was a religious belief, not a scientific theory. In November 2005, the board of education voted that evolution could be taught as a theory but not a fact. Also, intelligent design had to be presented as another possibility. However, in 2007, the board rejected the changed standards and returned to the previous ones.

The Brown sisters sit outside Monroe Elementary, a segregated school in Topeka, in 1953.

Local Government

Many decisions in Kansas are made at the local level. The state has 105 counties, each of which has its own government. Within those counties are cities and townships that may also have governments.

A group of people called commissioners runs county governments. They make laws that affect people in that area. Cities may have a mayor, a city council or commission, or some combination of both. Police and fire departments, school districts, and public health agencies are run by local governments. Certain roads, airports, or museums also come under local control.

In 1960, Kansas passed a law called the Constitutional Home Rule Amendment. This gave cities the power to make their own decisions, without asking the state's permission. However, a law at the local level cannot go against a law at the state level.

Sometimes it is not clear who is in charge. Two or more local governments may overlap in their duties. For example, Kansas City, Kansas, is a large city located in Wyandotte County. The city and county governments decided they would be more efficient if they worked together. In 1997, they became the state's first combined city/county government.

In total, Kansas has about four thousand different local governments. Clearly, Kansans like to do things their own way!

Politics in Kansas

Historically, Kansas has been a "red state." This means most people in Kansas vote for candidates in the Republican Party. (States that are predominantly Democratic are called blue states.) When Kansas first wrote its constitution, Republicans had more power. In fact, not

As a prank, Susanne Madora Salter's name was put on the ballot for mayor. However, Salter agreed to serve if she won, and paved the way for women in government.

a single Democrat voted for the state's new constitution. Today, Republicans are still the majority in Kansas. There have been thirty-six presidential elections since Kansas became a state. Only seven times have Kansans not voted for the Republican candidate. The last time was almost fifty years ago—in 1964. However, since 1967, the state has had more Democratic governors than Republican ones. Governor Mark Parkinson used to be a Republican but became a Democrat when he ran for office with former governor Kathleen Sebelius.

Kansas's government has always been open to women. Women were allowed to vote in local elections as early as 1887. In 1912, the state ruled that women could vote in state elections as well. That was before women in other parts of the country were allowed to vote at all. Women could also hold office. In 1887, a woman was elected mayor in Argonia, Kansas. She was the first woman mayor in the country!

Chapter 4

THE ECONOMY OF KANSAS

If you had a sandwich or cookies with your lunch, there is a good chance that a Kansas farmer had something to do with it. Flour comes from wheat, and Kansas grows more wheat than any other state in the nation. The state is sometimes called America's breadbasket. The Kansas economy also depends on energy, aviation, and service industries such as health and education.

Natural Resources

Early settlers in Kansas did not grow much wheat. They grew corn instead. However, the Kansas crop scene changed in 1874 when German immigrants from Russia arrived. They did not know how to grow corn. Instead, they planted a type of wheat called turkey red. This type of wheat grew in the winter, rather than the summer. It did well in the Kansas climate. These immigrants planted the seeds of Kansas's future. Now almost 9 million acres (4 million ha) of land in Kansas are devoted to growing wheat!

Other crops in Kansas include corn, alfalfa, barley, sunflowers, and soybeans. Grain sorghum is another crop. It is used to feed livestock. This is good because Kansas has a lot of livestock. There are more than six million head of cattle, and hogs are raised as well.

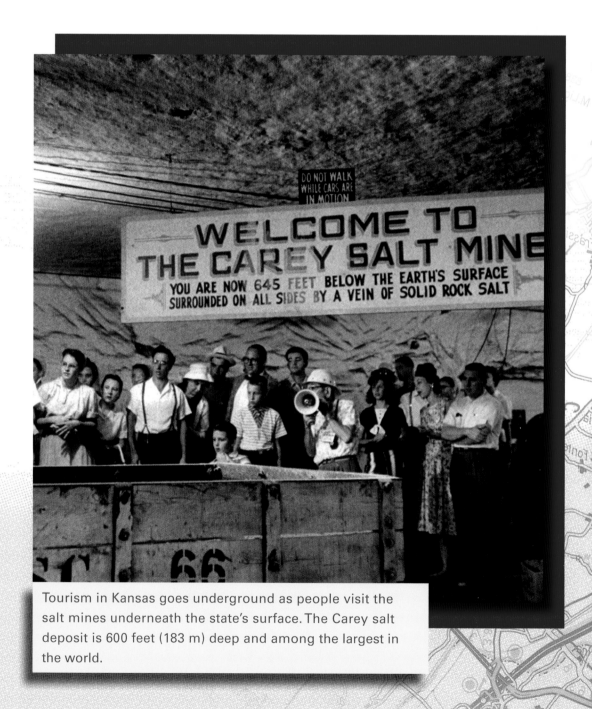

Tourism in Kansas goes underground as people visit the salt mines underneath the state's surface. The Carey salt deposit is 600 feet (183 m) deep and among the largest in the world.

Mining is another part of the Kansas economy. Underneath all that grass are minerals such as lead, zinc, coal, and limestone. The state also produces clay, shale, cement, and crushed rock. Hutchinson, Kansas, is home to a huge underground mountain of salt—the largest in the world. This salt isn't for eating. Instead, it is used to melt ice on roads and to make ice cream (it helps the freezing process). The Hutchinson Salt Mine has another purpose, too. The temperature underground doesn't change: It's 68°F (20°C) all year round. That makes it an ideal place to store the original reels of movies. *Gone with the Wind* is there, and so is *The Wizard of Oz*, of course. Dorothy is back in Kansas for good.

Aviation

With its wide-open sky, Kansas is a great place for flying. The aerospace industry started in Kansas in the early 1900s. Elaborate designs for flying machines emerged in the late 1800s and early 1900s. Many of these were never built. Some were built but never flew.

However, the ingenuity was there, and success would soon follow. In 1911, Kansan Clyde Cessna built a monoplane—one with only one layer of wings. Cessna didn't invent this idea, but he did perfect it. He started a company in Wichita to manufacture these airplanes. Other aviation pioneers, such as Walter Beech and William Lear, also started companies. Lear became known for making private luxury jets. Some of these companies are still in business. There are many new ones as well.

During World War II, Wichita companies began making parts for military airplanes. Military construction is still a large part of the aerospace industry in Wichita. People there build sections of commercial airplanes, too. A pilot training school and a research facility

Energy in Kansas

In 1860, an important Kansas journalist named George Washington Brown built the state's very first oil well. However, he did not get much oil out of it, and the Civil War stopped his efforts. In 1892, Standard Oil drilled the first commercial oil well west of the Mississippi River. Then in 1915, workers struck oil in El Dorado, Kansas. At the time, it was the biggest strike ever in the country. Soon the state was one of the country's biggest sources of oil. Western Kansas also had large amounts of natural gas. By 1938, more than half the state's counties were producing oil. Just six western counties combined produced enough oil to serve the whole country! Oil and natural gas are still an important part of the economy.

Wind blows hard through the plains of Kansas. Fortunately, all that power can be used. Giant windmills called turbines catch the wind and use it to make electricity. These turbines can be more than 400 feet (122 m) tall. The three blades are about 45 feet (14 m) long, and the central pivot is as big as a school bus. The biggest onshore turbines in the country are near the town of Concordia. There are 67 turbines producing 201 megawatts of power. That's enough to power sixty thousand homes a year!

Kansas already uses wind power for companies within the state. Now it's working to build more wind farms to serve neighboring states like Colorado. One challenge is to move all that energy. The state is working to build lines that can carry electricity into populated areas. Governor Mark Parkinson made a goal to have 20 percent of the state's electricity come from renewable energy sources—including wind—by 2020.

are located in Wichita. The city is called the Air Capital of the World. About half of all planes flying in the world today—from personal aircraft to fighter jets—were built in Kansas.

Other Industries

Most Kansans work in service industries. Instead of manufacturing a product, people who work in these industries provide a service. Service industries include health care, financial services, education, retail businesses, and gov-

Clyde Cessna was an early twentieth century aviator. His work on small, personal airplanes was one of the first steps in making Kansas a leader in the commercial aviation industry today.

ernment. Teachers, doctors, firemen, and store clerks are all service workers. Several national companies are based in Kansas, including Payless Shoes, Applebee's, and the Coleman Company, which makes camping equipment.

The state is working to bring in new industries. In the early 2000s, Kansas promoted itself as a place for biotechnology. Biotechnology involves studying living organisms. This research is used to develop products, such as medicine. Universities and private companies work together to do biotech research and development.

Grain elevators tower over the trees on the Kansas prairie, which produces more than three hundred million bushels of wheat each year. Wheat is stored inside the elevators before it is shipped to other places.

Rural citizens have heavily influenced Kansas's history, culture, and economy. The Kansas Department of Commerce recently formed the Office of Rural Opportunity. This office works with communities of fewer than five thousand people. It helps residents plan their communities and develop pride in them. This will help them attract businesses.

The Kansas economy reaches from tiny towns to foreign countries. Canada, Mexico, and Japan all import Kansas's products. Aircraft, other machinery, and cereals (which include wheat) are the largest exports. More than $12 billion worth of goods were sold internationally in 2008, almost double what they were a decade earlier. Those numbers fell in 2009 when the entire country entered a recession. However, the state's economy stayed strong overall.

Chapter 5

PEOPLE FROM KANSAS:
PAST AND PRESENT

Hundreds of years ago, Native Americans in central Kansas dug a long shallow trench in the shape of a snake. In northern Kansas, stones are arranged into a human figure called Penokee Man. Native Americans may have made this primitive art. Today, Kansas has another "earth artist." Stan Herd has created enormous works of art by plowing and planting fields into giant pictures that can be viewed from airplanes.

These people have left visible marks on Kansas. Many others have influenced the state in additional ways.

Writers, Artists, Musicians, and Actors

Melissa Etheridge (1961–) One of many musicians to come from Kansas is Melissa Etheridge. Her rock ballads are known all over the world. Etheridge writes music and sings, and she has won several major music awards.

Langston Hughes (1902–1967) Langston Hughes, an African American writer, spent his early childhood in Lawrence, Kansas. He would go on to become famous as a

Poet Langston Hughes lived in Kansas as a child. As an adult in New York, Hughes was an important part of the Harlem Renaissance in the 1920s, a movement that celebrated African American culture.

poet in the 1920s. Hughes was one of the first to compose in a style called jazz poetry, which used musical rhythms.

Hattie McDaniel (1895–1952) Actress Hattie McDaniel was the first black performer to win an Academy Award, which she received for her role in the 1939 classic movie *Gone with the Wind*.

Charlie Parker (1920–1955) Charlie Parker grew up in Kansas City, Kansas. Born in 1920, Parker composed music and revolutionized the way that the saxophone could be played. Nicknamed Bird, Parker became one of the most influential jazz musicians.

Gordon Parks (1912–2006) Gordon Parks scored a first for African Americans by becoming Hollywood's first major black director. He had a hit with the 1971 film *Shaft*. Parks also worked as a writer, photographer, and musician.

William Allen White (1868–1944) In the late 1800s, a Kansas man named William Allen White became known as a spokesman for Middle America. He was an author and a prize-winning journalist who was friends with U.S. presidents and regular people. Today, a national award for children's books is named after him.

Wild Westerners

Mabel Chase (1876-1962) In southern Kansas, Mabel Chase became the country's first female sheriff when she was

Home on the Range

In Kansas, you never know who your neighbor will be because Kansans are always on the move. In 1854, several men in Massachusetts formed the Emigrant Aid Company. It helped about two thousand people move from the North to the Kansas territory. The idea was to fill the state with people who opposed slavery. In response, proslavery people moved to Kansas from the Southern states. Later, in 1862, the federal government passed the Homestead Act. This gave free land to people willing to live on it. The act brought even more people to Kansas.

After the Civil War, immigrants began arriving from Europe, especially from Germany and Russia. African Americans came from the South. The population grew fast, and the state was filling up. In 1887, Wichita was the fastest-growing city in the nation. Towns often competed to become the county seat—the capital of the county. Boomtowns sprang up as new railroads and the cattle industry created instant communities.

Many boomtowns are now ghost towns. At the Kansas State Historical Society, there are shelves of notebooks filled with the names of "dead towns." The list has thousands of towns that died out when people moved away to seek better opportunities. Today, more people are moving out of Kansas than moving into it. And within the state, many are choosing to live in the cities, rather than in rural areas.

In the early 2000s, some towns started to fight back. They offered residents free land that they could live on, as well as tax breaks and money to help pay for their houses. To seal the deal, the towns assured newcomers that their new homes would get high-speed Internet.

elected in 1926. She drove an armor-plated car with bulletproof windows, and she carried a submachine gun. Bank robbers and bootleggers had to beware!

Wyatt Earp (1848–1929)
In the 1870s, Wyatt Earp served as a marshal (also known as a sheriff) in Wichita and Dodge City, Kansas. He is legendary for his success in bringing murderers and gangs of thieves to justice. In Dodge City, Earp teamed up with Bat Masterson, another famous local lawman. James "Wild Bill" Hickok, who was known for his skill with a gun, also worked as a lawman during the Wild West days in the state of Kansas.

Kansan Charles Curtis, who was part Native American, became the first non-Caucasian person to serve in a high U.S. office. He was vice president under President Herbert Hoover.

Politicians and Activists

John Brown (1800–1859) A century and a half after John Brown's death, historians still debate whether he was a hero or a criminal. Brown battled hard against slavery, but his violent methods caught up with him. In 1859, he attacked a

More than seventy years after she disappeared over the Pacific Ocean, the aviator Amelia Earhart still captures people's imaginations, and people continue to look for the wreckage of her plane.

federal armory in Virginia. He was captured, tried, and found guilty. He was hanged on December 2, 1859.

Charles Curtis (1860–1936) In 1929, Charles Curtis became vice president under President Herbert Hoover. He was part Native American. Until Barack Obama, Curtis was the only president or vice president with a non-European background.

Robert Dole (1923–) Another important politician from Kansas is Robert Dole. Dole ran for president in 1996 but was defeated by Bill Clinton. In 2003, the Robert J. Dole Institute of Politics was opened at the University of Kansas.

Carrie Nation (1846–1911) Carrie Nation had a different cause: prohibition. She had been married to an alcoholic husband, so she was determined to fight against drinking. She actually used a hatchet to smash up saloons! Some of them put up signs that read: "All Nations Welcome But Carrie."

Legends

Amelia Earhart (1897–1937?) Amelia Earhart, from Atchison, was a popular female pilot. In 1932, Earhart became the first woman to fly solo across the Atlantic Ocean. In 1937, she decided to fly around the world with her navigator, Fred Noonan. They almost made it. However, somewhere over the South Pacific, Earhart lost radio contact and the plane vanished. Earhart and Noonan were never seen again, and the plane has never been found.

James Naismith (1861–1939) Kansans are passionate about basketball. In 1898, a man named James Naismith came to Kansas and started a basketball program at the University of Kansas. Naismith had invented the game only seven years earlier. His idea paid off: The university's basketball program is now one of the best in the country.

Timeline

1541	Spanish explorer Francisco Vásquez de Coronado looks for a city of gold in Kansas.
1804	Lewis and Clark travel through Kansas.
1806	Zebulon Pike explores Kansas.
1821	The Santa Fe Trail is established.
1854	The Kansas-Nebraska Act opens Kansas to white settlement.
1856	Violence erupts between abolitionists and proslavery forces.
1859	Abolitionist John Brown is found guilty after raiding a federal armory; he is hanged.
1861	Kansas becomes a state; the Civil War begins.
1863	William Quantrill raids Lawrence and burns the city.
1860s	Railroads and the cattle industry expand and help the development of frontier Kansas.
1874	Immigrants bring turkey red wheat to Kansas.
1879	About six thousand southern blacks, called Exodusters, move to Kansas.
1915	The largest oil well in the country is established near El Dorado, Kansas.
1920s	The aviation industry begins to grow in Wichita.
1930s	The Dust Bowl ruins many Kansas farmers.
1954	The U.S. Supreme Court rules against segregation in *Brown vs. Board of Education*.
2001	Kansas's first commercial wind farm is built in Gray County.
2005	The theory of intelligent design becomes part of the state science curriculum.
2007	An F-5 tornado severely damages Greensburg, Kansas.
2008	Kansas sets a state record with $12.5 billion in exports.
2009	Governor Kathleen Sebelius resigns to join President Barack Obama's cabinet.

State motto:	*Ad astra per aspera* ("To the stars through difficulties")
State capital:	Topeka
State tree:	Cottonwood
State bird:	Western meadowlark
State flower:	Sunflower
Statehood date and number:	January 29, 1861; thirty-fourth state
State nicknames:	Sunflower State, Wheat State, Free State
Total area and U.S. rank:	82,282 square miles (213,109 sq kilometers); fifteenth-largest state
Population:	2,688,000
Highest elevation:	Mount Sunflower, at 4,039 feet (1,231 m)
Lowest elevation:	Verdigris River, at 680 feet (207 m)

State flag

State seal

Major rivers:	Arkansas River, Kansas (Kaw) River, Verdigris River, Neosho River, Solomon River, Smoky Hill River
Major lakes:	Tuttle Creek, John Redmond Reservoir, Milford Lake, Cedar Bluff Lake
Highest recorded temperature:	121°F (49°C) at Alton, on July 18, 1936
Coldest recorded temperature:	-40°F (-4°C) at Lebanon, on February 13, 1905
Origin of state name:	Named after the Kansa tribe of Native Americans
Chief agricultural products:	Wheat, livestock, sorghum, soybeans
Major industries:	Agriculture, aviation, petroleum

Western meadowlark

Sunflower

GLOSSARY

adaptable Flexible; able to change when necessary.

armory A place where weapons are stored.

bill A draft of a law.

devastate To severely damage.

elaborate Very fancy or detailed.

eligible To qualify; to meet the requirements for something.

immigrant A person who moves to a new place and becomes a permanent part of the community.

ingenuity Creativity and skill in making something.

integrate To include people of all races.

legendary Having great fame and influence.

primitive Basic; unsophisticated.

prohibition Not allowing people to drink alcoholic beverages.

promote To encourage the use of something.

recession A downturn in the economy.

renewable Easily grown, produced, or manufactured.

secede To break away.

segregate To separate people of different races.

thrive To flourish or do well.

unanimous Having complete agreement; without any dissent.

zealous Extremely committed or passionate about something.

FOR MORE INFORMATION

Kansas Aviation Museum

3350 South George Washington Boulevard

Wichita, KS 67210

(316) 683-9242

Web site: http://www.kansasaviationmuseum.org

The Kansas Aviation Museum has extensive exhibits with information about the history of aviation in Kansas.

Kansas Department of Commerce

1000 SW Jackson Street, Suite 100

Topeka, KS 66612-1354

(785) 296-3481

Web site: http://www.kansascommerce.com

This department works to create jobs, encourage community development, and bring business to Kansas.

Kansas Department of Wildlife and Parks

512 SE 25th Avenue

Pratt, KS 67124

(620) 672-5911

Web site: http://www.kdwp.state.ks.us

The Kansas Department of Wildlife and Parks manages the state's natural resources and offers educational programs.

Kansas Sampler Foundation

978 Arapaho Road

Inman, KS 67546

(620) 585-2374

Web site: http://www.kansassampler.org

The Kansas Sampler Foundation is devoted to preserving and promoting rural culture in Kansas.

Kansas State Historical Society

6425 SW 6th Avenue

Topeka, KS 66615

(785) 272-8681

Web site: http://www.kshs.org

The society works to preserve Kansas's history by collecting materials and providing educational assistance.

Office of the Governor

Capitol Building

300 SW 10th Avenue, Suite 212S

Topeka, KS 66612-1590

(877) 579-6757

Web site: http://www.governor.ks.gov

The governor's office is the head of Kansas's executive branch.

University of Kansas

Lawrence, KS 66045

(785) 864-2700

Web site: http://www.ku.edu

Kansas's largest public university has several programs relating to the state's history, geography, and geology.

Web Sites

Due to the changing nature of Internet links, Rosen Publishing has developed an online list of Web sites related to the subject of this book. This site is updated regularly. Please use this link to access the list:

http://www.rosenlinks.com/uspp/kspp

Bjorklund, Ruth, and Trudi Strain Trueit. *Kansas*. Tarrytown, NY: Marshall Cavendish Benchmark, 2009.

Bograd, Larry. *Uniquely Kansas*. Chicago, IL: Heinemann-Raintree, 2005.

Cannarella, Deborah. *Kansas*. New York, NY: Children's Press, 2008.

Chu, Daniel, and Bill Shaw. *Going Home to Nicodemus: The Story of an African American Frontier Town and the Pioneers Who Settled It*. Morristown, NJ: Julian Messner, 1994.

Cutchins, Judy, and Ginny Johnston. *Giant Predators of the Ancient Seas*. Sarasota, FL: Pineapple Press, 2001.

Gordon, Sherri Mabry. *The Evolution Debate: Darwinism vs. Intelligent Design*. Berkeley Heights, NJ: Enslow Publishers, 2009.

Grant, Reg. *Slavery*. New York, NY: DK Children, 2009.

Hinton, Kaavonia. *Brown vs. Board of Education of Topeka, Kansas, 1954*. Hockessin, DE: Mitchell Lane Publishers, 2009.

Ingram, Scott. *Kansas*. New York, NY: Children's Press, 2009.

Jennings, Richard. *Ghost Town*. New York, NY: Houghton Mifflin Books for Children, 2009.

Klaassen, Mike. *The Brute*. Port Orchard, WA: Blue Works, 2005.

Kochenderfer, Lee. *The Victory Garden*. New York, NY: Delacorte Books for Young Readers, 2002.

McArthur, Debra. *The Kansas-Nebraska Act and Bleeding Kansas in American History*. Berkeley Heights, NJ: Enslow Publishers, 2003.

Murray, Stuart. *Wild West*. New York, NY: DK Children, 2005.

Netzley, Patricia. *Seeds of a Nation—Kansas*. Farmington Hills, MI: KidHaven, 2002.

Olien, Rebecca. *Kansas*. Mankato, MN: Capstone, 2003.

O'Neal, Claire. *How to Use Wind Power to Light and Heat Your Home*. Hockessin, DE: Mitchell Lane Publishers, 2009.

Patent, Dorothy Hinshaw. *The Buffalo and the Indians: A Shared Destiny*. New York, NY: Clarion Books, 2006.

Sanford, William. *The Chisholm Trail in American History*. Berkeley Heights, NJ: Enslow Publishers, 2000.

Silverstein, Alvin, Virginia Silverstein, and Laura Silverstein Nunn. *Tornadoes: The Science Behind Terrible Twisters*. Berkeley Heights, NJ: Enslow Publishers, 2009.

Stanley, George E. *Dwight D. Eisenhower: Young Military Leader*. New York, NY: Aladdin, 2006.

Stone, Tanya. *Amelia Earhart*. New York, NY: DK Children, 2007.

Swanson, Wayne. *Why the West Was Wild*. Toronto, ON: Annick Press, 2004.

Thomas, Joyce Carol. *Linda Brown, You are Not Alone: the Brown vs. Board of Education Decision*. New York, NY: Hyperion, 2003.

Thomas, William. *Kansas*. Milwaukee, WI: Gareth Stevens Publishing, 2006.

Trescott, Matty. *The Town on Rambling Creek*. Manchester, NH: Smith and Kraus, 2004.

Wallace, Maurice. *Langston Hughes: The Harlem Renaissance*. New York, NY: Benchmark Books, 2008.

Williams, Jeanne. *Winter Wheat*. Bloomington, IN: iUniverse, 2000.

Winn, Kimberly. *Local Government in Kansas*. Topeka, KS: LKM, 2005.

Woog, Adam. *Wyatt Earp*. New York, NY: Chelsea House, 2010.

Young, Jeff. *Bleeding Kansas and the Violent Clash Over Slavery in the Heartland*. Berkeley Heights, NJ: Enslow Publishers, 2006.

BIBLIOGRAPHY

Buchanan, Rex, ed. *Kansas Geology*. Lawrence, KS: University Press of Kansas, 1984.

Collins, Joseph T., ed. *Natural Kansas*. Lawrence, KS: University Press of Kansas, 1985.

Dary, David. *More True Tales of Old-Time Kansas*. Lawrence, KS: University Press of Kansas, 1987.

Dean, Virgil W., ed. *Territorial Kansas Reader*. Topeka, KS: Kansas State Historical Society, 2005.

DeLano, Patti. *Kansas: Off the Beaten Path*. Guilford, CT: Globe Pequot Press, 2005.

Everhart, Michael. *Oceans of Kansas: A Natural History of the Western Interior Sea*. Bloomington, IN: Indiana University Press, 2005.

Fitzgerald, Daniel. *Faded Dreams: More Ghost Towns of Kansas*. Lawrence, KS: University Press of Kansas, 1994.

Grout, Pam. *Kansas Curiosities: Quirky Characters, Roadside Oddities & Other Offbeat Stuff*. Guilford, CT: Globe Pequot Press, 2006.

Hann, David. *Kansas Past: Pieces of the 34th Star*. Lawrence, KS: Penthe Publishing, 1999.

Hoard, Robert J., and William E. Banks, eds. *Kansas Archaeology*. Lawrence, KS: University Press of Kansas, 2006.

Hoy, Jim. *Flint Hills Cowboys*. Lawrence, KS: University Press of Kansas, 2006.

Kansas Department of Commerce, Trade Development Division. "2008 Kansas Export Statistics." Retrieved July 13, 2009 (http://www.kansascommerce.com/LinkClick. aspx?fileticket = ibbFp6sUcUU = &tabid = 89).

Kansas Geological Survey. "Geologic Regions." Retrieved August 13, 2009 (http://www. kgs.ku.edu/Extension/home.html).

Kansas Geological Survey. "Industrial Minerals in Kansas." Fall 1999. Retrieved July 13, 2009 (http://www.kgs.ku.edu/Magellan/Minerals/industrial.html).

Kansas Sampler Foundation. "Wichita Aviation Industry." Retrieved August 10, 2009 (http://www.kansassampler.org/8wonders/commerce.php?id = 31).

Kansas State Historical Society. "Topics in Kansas History: Old West." Retrieved July 2, 2009 (http://www.kshs.org/research/topics/oldwest/essay.htm).

Max, Sarah. "Free Land in the Heartland." CNNMoney.com, December 23, 2004. Retrieved July 2, 2009 (http://money.cnn.com/2004/12/22/real_estate/buying_ selling/thursday_freeland).

Metz, Christine. "State Poised to Capitalize on Renewable Energy." *Lawrence Journal-World*, June 19, 2009, p. 1A.

Metz, Christine. "Wind Farm Invigorates Rural Area." *Lawrence Journal-World*, June 20, 2009, p. 1A.

Miner, Craig. *Kansas: The History of the Sunflower State*. Lawrence, KS: University Press of Kansas, 2002.

Miner, Craig. *West of Wichita*. Lawrence, KS: University Press of Kansas, 1986.

Nature Conservancy. "Tallgrass Prairie National Preserve." Retrieved July 11, 2009 (http://www.nature.org/wherewework/northamerica/states/kansas/preserves/art15403.html).

Reichman, O. J. *Living Landscapes of Kansas*. Lawrence, KS: University Press of Kansas, 1995.

Rowe, Frank Joseph, and Craig Miner. *Borne on the South Wind: A Century of Aviation in Kansas*. Wichita, KS: Wichita Eagle and Beacon Publishing Co., 1994.

Shortridge, James R. *Peopling the Plains: Who Settled Where in Frontier Kansas*. Lawrence, KS: University Press of Kansas, 1995.

Skelton, Lawrence H. "A Brief History of the Kansas Oil and Gas Industry." Petroleum History Institute. Retrieved July 13, 2009 (http://www.petroleumhistory.org/journalvol7.html).

INDEX

About the Author

Diane Bailey lives in Lawrence, Kansas, only a few miles from where the early battles over slavery were fought. She has been through tornadoes, collected fossils, and walked through fields of wheat and sunflowers. When she's not outside enjoying Kansas, Bailey is inside writing on a variety of nonfiction topics.

Photo Credits

Cover (top left) Archive Holdings, Inc./Getty Images; cover (top right) Larry W. Smith/ Getty Images; cover (bottom) Altrendo Nature/Getty Images; pp. 3, 6, 12, 18, 19, 23, 30, 37, 39 (right) Shutterstock.com; p. 4 (top) © GeoAtlas; p. 7 FPG/Hulton Archive/Getty Images; p. 9 © www.istockphoto.com/ClixPhoto; p. 10 Jim Watson/AFP/Getty Images; p. 11 Kyle Gerstner/America 24-7/Getty Images; p. 13 Transcendental Graphics/Hulton Archive/Getty Images; pp. 15, 31 MPI/Hulton Archive/Getty Images; p. 17 SSPL via Getty Images; pp. 20, 24 Carl Iwasaki/Time & Life Pictures/Getty Images; pp. 22, 27 KansasMemory.org, Kansas State Historical Society; p. 28 VisionsofAmerica/Joe Sohm/ Digital Vision/Getty Images; p. 34 Chicago History Museum/Hulton Archive/Getty Images; p. 35 Pictures, Inc./Time & Life Pictures/Getty Images; p. 38 (left) Courtesy of Robesus, Inc.; p. 39 (left) © www.istockphoto.com/Noah Strycker.

Designer: Les Kanturek; Editor: Bethany Bryan;
Photo Researcher: Peter Tomlinson